I Can DRAW
Things That Move

Cover illustrated by Eldon Doty
Interiors illustrated by George Gaadt

Here's what you need...

You're about to become an artist! Before you start, make sure you have a pencil, a pencil sharpener, an eraser, a felt-tip pen, and one or more of the different types of media pictured here. Then, look in the back of the book for your grid pages. They'll help you to follow the special drawing steps. If you need more paper, you can ask a grownup to help you to copy them.

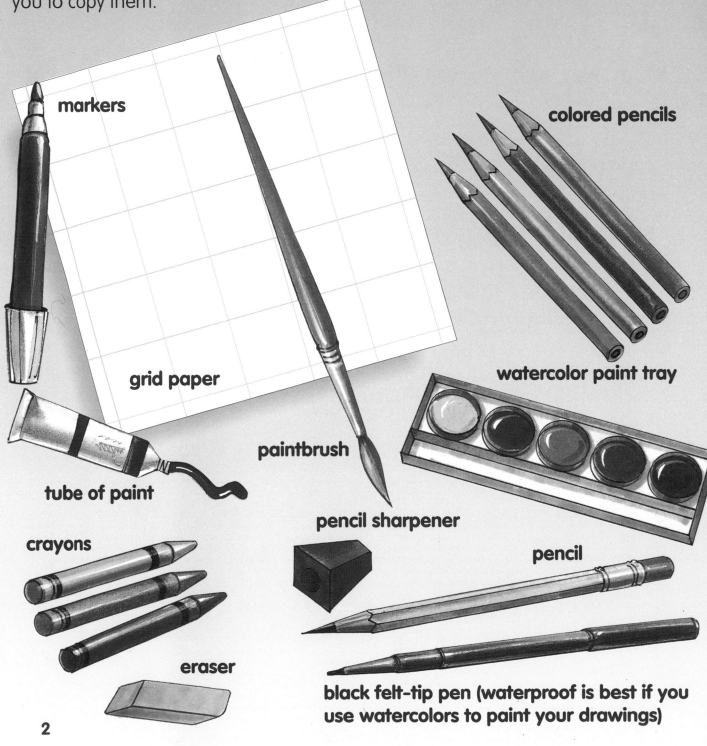

markers

colored pencils

grid paper

watercolor paint tray

tube of paint

paintbrush

pencil sharpener

crayons

pencil

eraser

black felt-tip pen (waterproof is best if you use watercolors to paint your drawings)

2

And here's what you do!

1 Copy each step-by-step drawing onto your grid paper, noticing where the drawing should touch the lines on your grid. Draw lightly in pencil. Since each new step is shown in blue, you'll always know exactly what to do next.

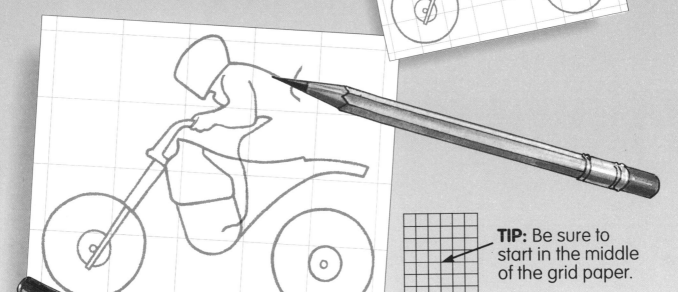

TIP: Be sure to start in the middle of the grid paper.

2 You may erase the pencil construction lines as you go along so that you can see how your drawing is progressing. When you have finished, use your felt-tip pen to go over the lines you want to keep, and erase any stray pencil lines.

Now you have a perfect drawing to color any way you'd like! Before you color, you may want to read pages 30-32 for some extra coloring tips.

3

Bomber

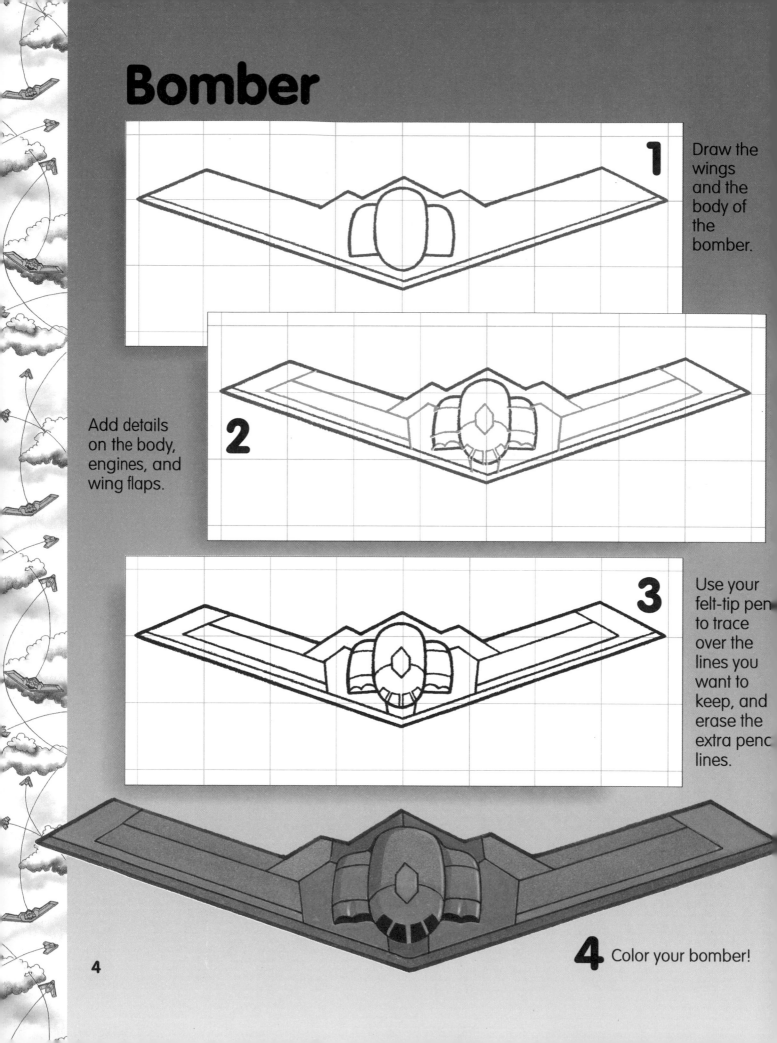

1 Draw the wings and the body of the bomber.

Add details on the body, engines, and wing flaps. **2**

3 Use your felt-tip pen to trace over the lines you want to keep, and erase the extra pencil lines.

4 Color your bomber!

4

Blimp

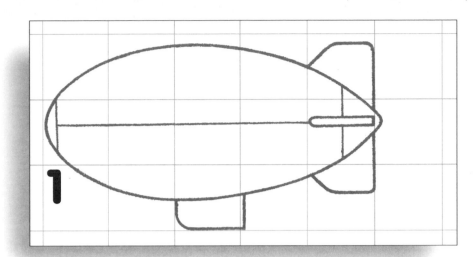

Draw the body, the tail, and passenger cabin.

1

2 Add curved lines to the body and flaps on the tail. Draw windows and a propeller on the cabin.

Use your felt-tip pen to trace over the lines you want to keep, and erase the extra pencil lines.

3

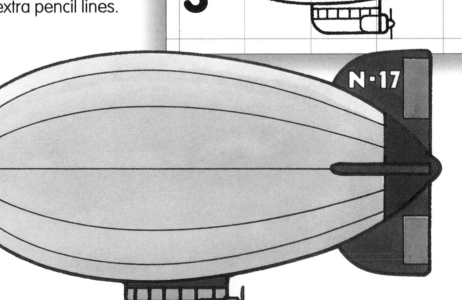

N·17

4 Color your blimp!

Motorcycle

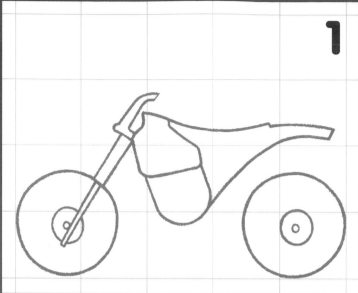

1 Draw the main engine body, handlebar, and wheels. Draw straight lines to connect the front wheel to the handlebar.

Draw the rider leaning forward over the handlebar. Add a footrest, details on the engine, and connect the rear wheel to the body.

2

3 Draw the fender over the front tire, and add details to the driver's helmet, the seat, the wheels, and the main engine body. Also draw a racing plate beside the seat.

4 Complete the details of your motorcycle and add a number to the racing plate. Give the rider a belt and elbow and knee pads.

Use your felt-tip pen to trace the lines you want to keep, and erase the pencil lines.

5

6 Color your motorcycle!

Shuttle

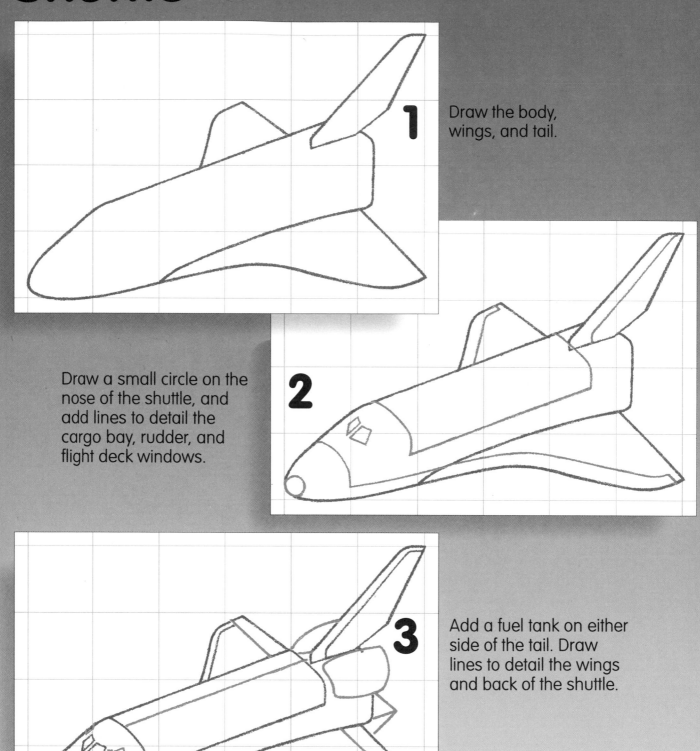

1 Draw the body, wings, and tail.

Draw a small circle on the nose of the shuttle, and add lines to detail the cargo bay, rudder, and flight deck windows.

2

3 Add a fuel tank on either side of the tail. Draw lines to detail the wings and back of the shuttle.

Draw the main engines behind the fuel tanks. Add more detail to the body, nose, and wings.

Use your felt-tip pen to trace over the lines you want to keep, and erase the extra pencil lines.

4

5

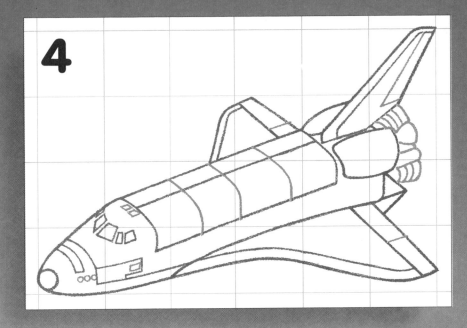

You can add numbers, letters, or create your own designs to draw on the wings of your space shuttle!

6 Color your shuttle!

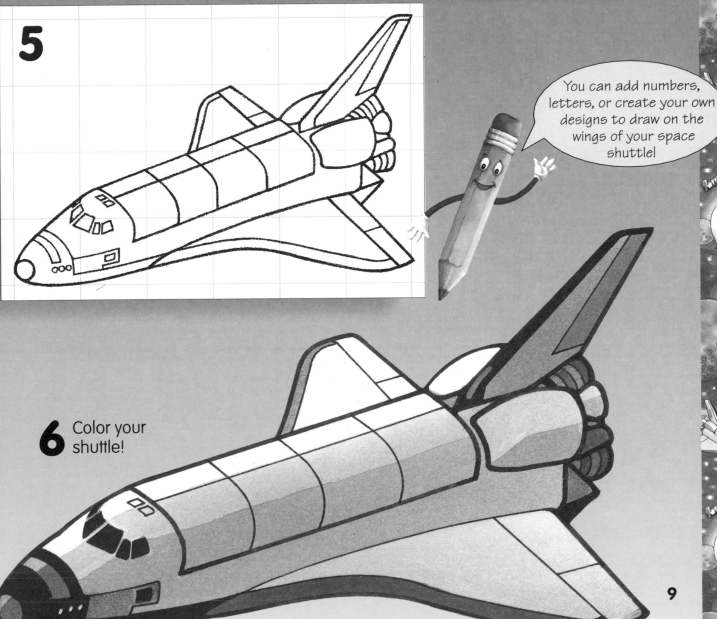

Saturn

palm tree

gravel

10

Making Backgrounds

You can add background scenery to make your pictures even more realistic. Backgrounds can add excitement that will make your drawings get noticed. Try copying the ones shown here, and then make up some of your own!

Learn to draw the Indy car on pages 16 and 17. ▲

Learn to draw the dump truck on pages 14 and 15.

Learn to draw the shuttle on pages 8 and 9. ▲

Learn to draw the schooner on pages 12 and 13. ▲

Schooner

Draw two overlapping triangular shapes for the sails. Also draw the basic shape of the hull.

1

Use straight lines for the masts and ropes. Draw two more sails curving inward.

2

Draw six more ropes and add a cabin and a railing.

3

4 Add flags, portholes, and curved ropes, and finish the railing.

Use your felt-tip pen to trace the lines you want to keep, and erase the extra pencil lines.

5

6 Color your schooner!

Dump Truck

Draw the cab, the wheels, and the dump body.

Draw ovals inside the wheels, and lines for the grill and cab door. Add details to the truck frame.

Add smaller ovals in the center of each wheel, draw the windows on the cab, and add details on the dump body.

4 Give your dump truck details on the grill and truck frame and add treads to the tires.

When drawing complex vehicles, it's a good idea to erase construction lines as you go along.

Use your felt-tip pen to trace the lines you want to keep, and erase the extra pencil lines.

5

6 Color your dump truck!

Indy Car

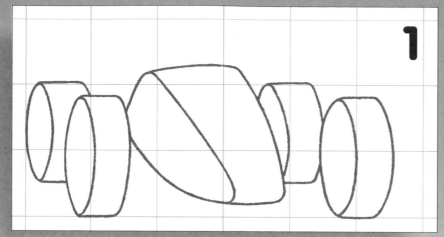

1 Draw a wedge shape for the body and add four wheels on the sides.

Draw the rear wing and add lines to connect the body to the wheels.

2

3 Draw the front wing, side pod details, wheel ovals, and driver's helmet.

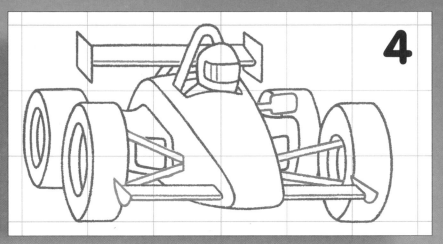

4 Draw suspension struts to connect the wheels to the body. Add details to front and rear wings, and draw side-view mirror.

Use your felt-tip pen to trace the lines you want to keep, and erase the extra pencil lines.

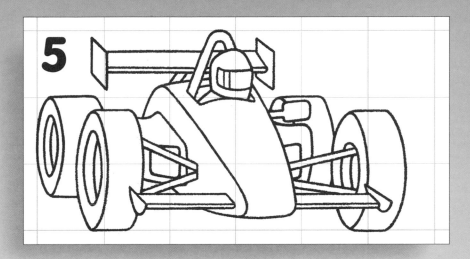

5

6 Color your Indy car!

Creating Action

Putting in brisk lines that show that something moves can add a sense of action and energy. Try quickly drawing several light strokes along the rear edge of your fast-moving vehicle, or behind the part of a machine that is moving. Use the lines to show the path your subject is taking—for instance, curved lines around the helicopter propellers, or long, swooping lines behind the bomber.

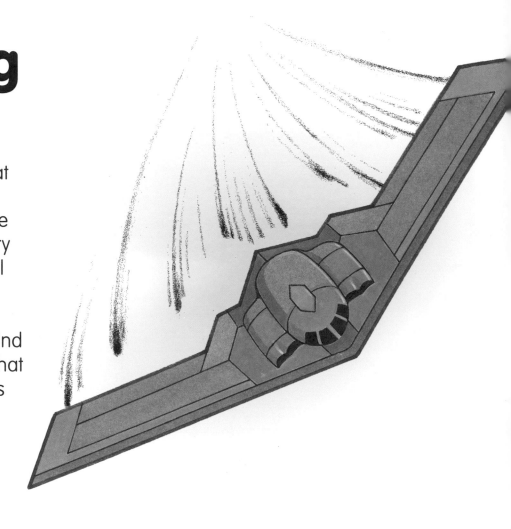

Locomotive

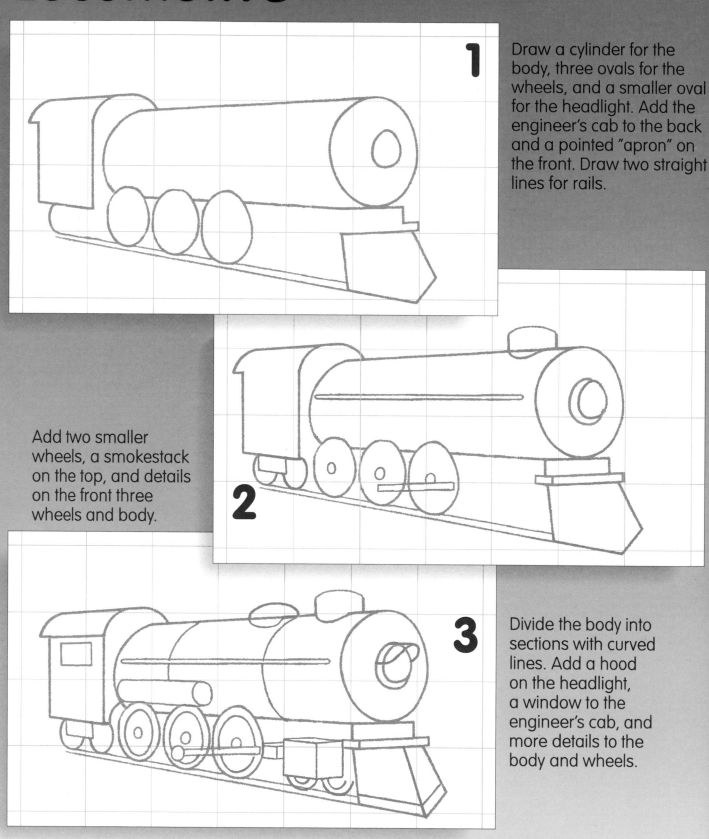

1 Draw a cylinder for the body, three ovals for the wheels, and a smaller oval for the headlight. Add the engineer's cab to the back and a pointed "apron" on the front. Draw two straight lines for rails.

Add two smaller wheels, a smokestack on the top, and details on the front three wheels and body.

2

3 Divide the body into sections with curved lines. Add a hood on the headlight, a window to the engineer's cab, and more details to the body and wheels.

Complete the details on the locomotive.

4

5 Use your felt-tip pen to trace the lines you want to keep, and erase the extra pencil lines.

You can draw the rest of the train cars by drawing rectangles instead of cylinders for the body, and leaving off the apron.

6 Color your locomotive!

Mega Wheels

Draw the body and the wheels.

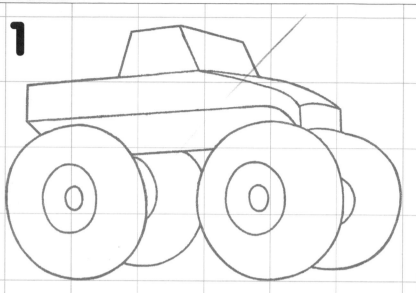

Draw the headlights and windows, and add details to the wheels.

Draw the door, two more headlights, and the axle. Add smaller ovals inside the wheels.

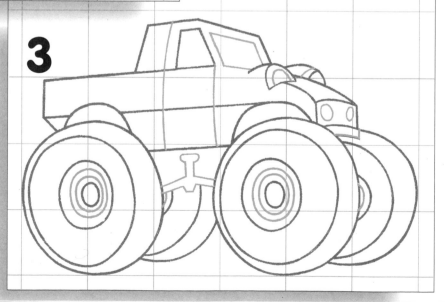

4 Add treads to the tires and small half-circles inside the headlights. Draw extra lines across the cab and door.

Use your felt-tip pen to trace the lines you want to keep, and erase the extra pencil lines.

5

Notice how the tires on Mega Wheels account for half of its height!

6 Color your Mega Wheels!

Putting It All Together

Once you've learned how to draw several vehicles, you can create an exciting scene like the one shown here. Notice how the motorcycle and dump truck can be seen close-up, and the schooner and helicopter appear to be further away. Practice drawing your vehicles at different angles and in different sizes. This will give your pictures depth and interest.

trees

building

24

clouds

Helicopter

Draw the cabin, tail, and landing skids.

1

Draw the windows and add curved lines to connect the landing skids to the cabin. Draw the main propellers' rotor head on the top.

2

Draw the main propellers and tail propeller support. Add curved lines to the top of the body.

3

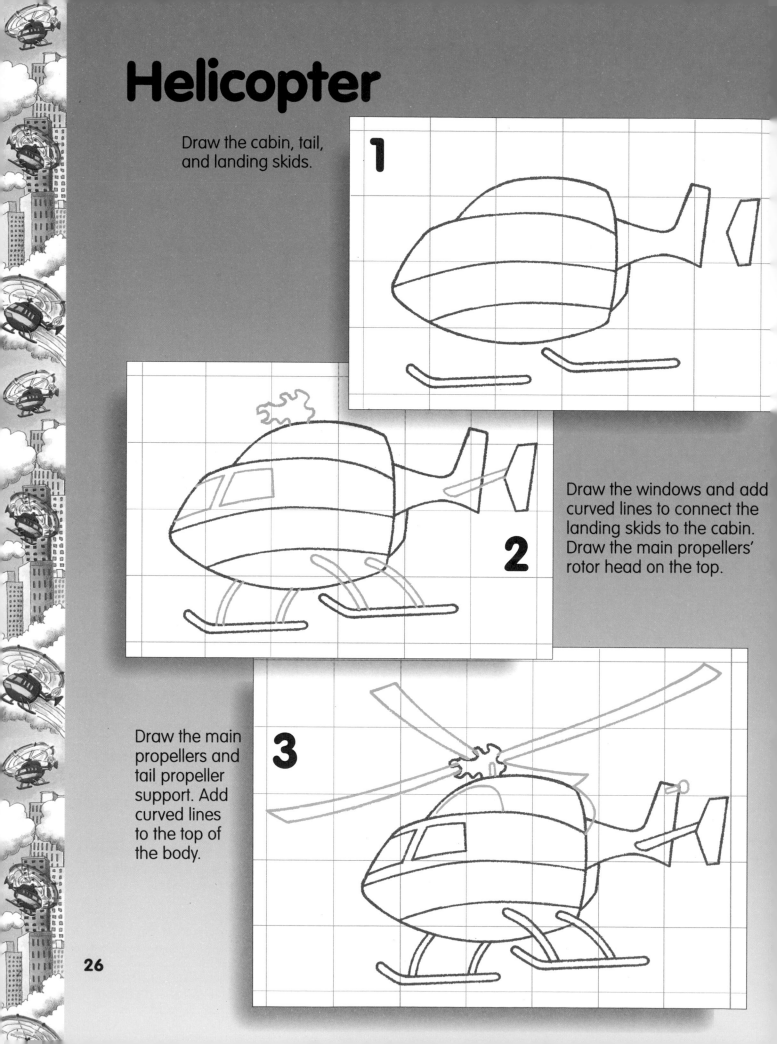

4 Draw more windows. Add a small propeller on the tail and further details.

Notice how the tail propeller appears to be moving. Turn to page 19 to learn how to make the overhead propellers move, too!

Use your felt-tip pen to trace the lines you want to keep, and erase the extra pencil lines.

5

6 Color your helicopter!

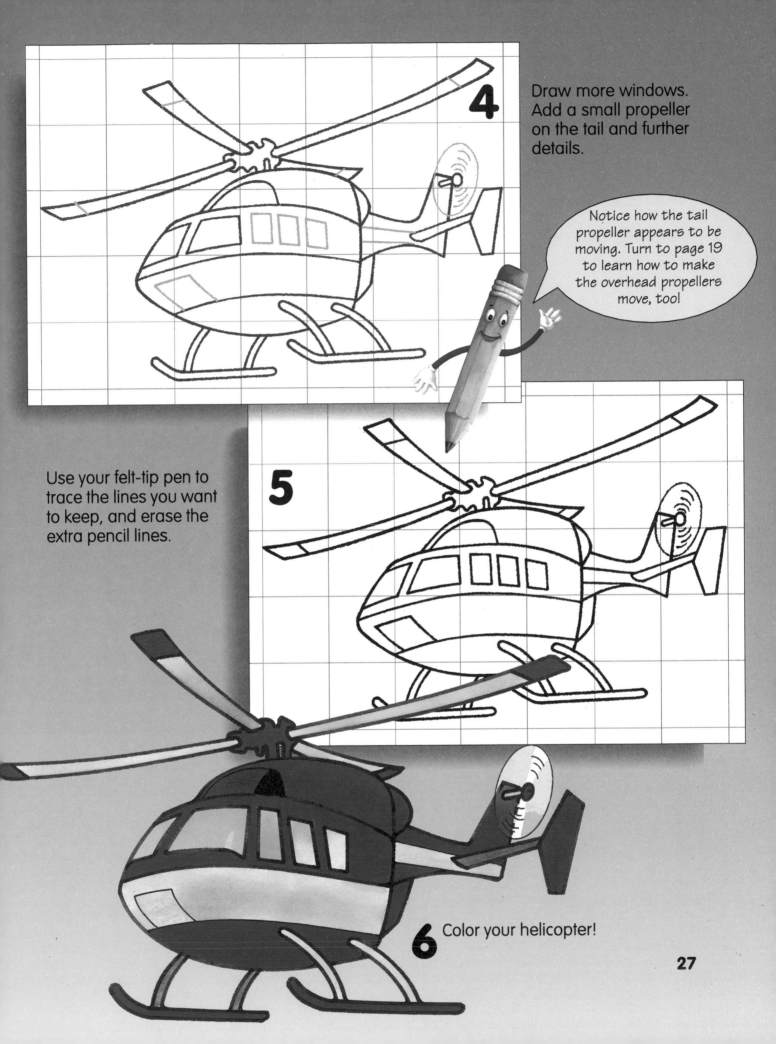

Bulldozer

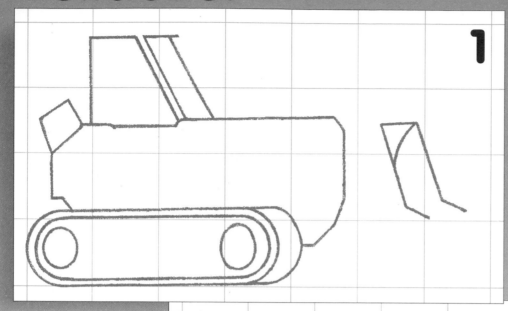

1 Draw the body, cab, and part of the front shovel. Connect the two wheels with a long capsule-shaped tire track.

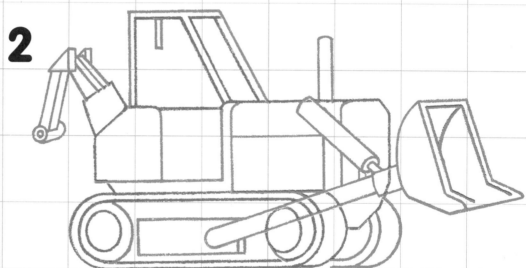

2 Add the door, lines around the hood, and the arm cylinder for the backhoe. Draw a tube for the exhaust pipe on the engine's hood. Add details to front shovel and body.

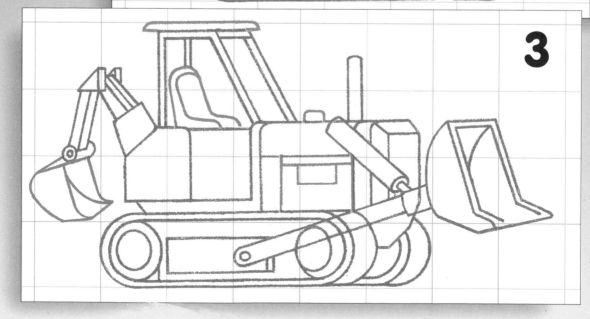

3 Add the driver's seat and the bucket on the backhoe.

4 Add short, straight lines to detail the grill, treads, seat, and shovels. You can fill the front shovel with bumpy lines and dots to look like dirt.

Use your felt-tip pen to trace the lines you want to keep, and erase the extra pencil lines.

5

6 Color your bulldozer!

Coloring Your Drawings

Once you've finished the outlines of your drawings, it's fun to color them in. Use watercolor paints, colored pencils, crayons, markers, or anything else you can think of!

Watercolors are fun to use, but sometimes when two wet paint colors are next to one another, they run together. If you're using watercolors, you might want to let the paint dry after each color you use.

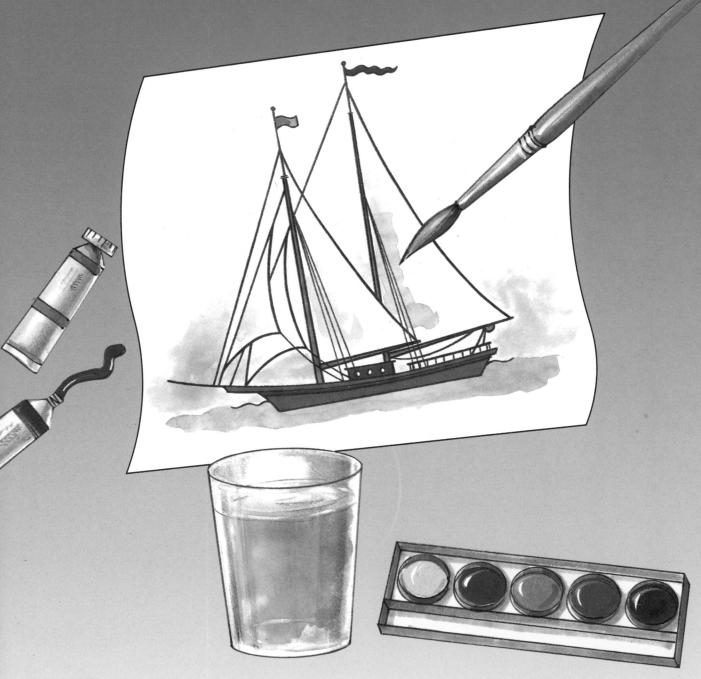

Turn to the next page to learn a really special way to bring your drawings to life!

Markers give your drawings a smooth, bright finish and even colors.

Crayons and colored pencils are good for shading. See page 32 to learn how!

Shading Your Drawings

Shading can add dimension and life to your drawings. Try shading first with a crayon or colored pencil. Make an area of your vehicle darker where there would be less light on the vehicle. Then add lighter color where the light would hit the vehicle, and watch your drawing come to life!

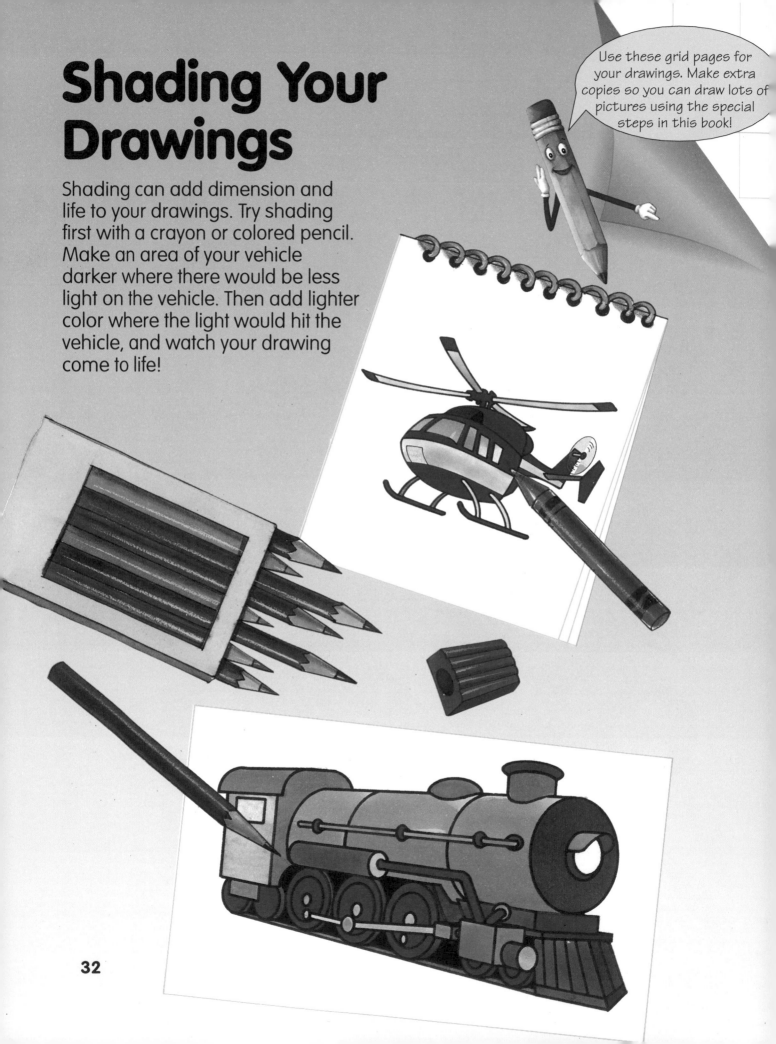

Use these grid pages for your drawings. Make extra copies so you can draw lots of pictures using the special steps in this book!